To Jonathan

From your fiance
Amelia almost **amelia's**
Wright **long**

journey

amelia's long journey

Stories about a brave girl
and her fight against cancer.

by her dad,
John L. Smith

Stephens Press ∗ Las Vegas, Nevada

Editor: Jami Carpenter
Book Designer: Sue Campbell
Project Coordinator: Stacey Fott
Cover Photo: Jim Laurie
Book Photos: Courtesy of Smith Family
Author photo: John Waldron

Cataloging in Publication
Smith, John L., 1960-
Amelia's long journey : stories about a brave girl and her fight against cancer / John L.
Smith.
212 p. : photos ; 15 cm.
ISBN: 1-935043-15-3
ISBN-13: 978-1-935043-15-7
Collected here are the newspaper columns written by columnist John L. Smith
concerning the treatment and recovery of his daughter, Amelia, who was diagnosed with
a cancerous brain tumor.
1. Smith, Amelia. 2. Cancer—Patients. I. Title.
616.99'4 dc 22 2009 2009936953

STEPHENS PRESS, LLC
A Stephens Media Company

Post Office Box 1600
Las Vegas, NV 89125-1600
www.stephenspress.com
Printed in United States of America

To our nurses, doctors, family, and friends.
You stand by us and help us
make the most of each day.

Amelia and her dad at the dinosaur show.

Acknowledgments

A few weeks after Amelia underwent surgery to remove a malignant brain tumor in October 2004, she appeared to have recovered fully and was responding well to chemotherapy. It was then a friend asked, "Are you going to write a book about this experience?"

I'd already thought about it and had been keeping notes between column deadlines and doctor visits. The intense pressure on our small family had been great, but the worst appeared to be over. The cancer that threatened our daughter's life seemed to be gone.

But when Amelia's cancer relapsed in May 2005, we were overwhelmed by anxiety and sorrow. I found it difficult to move, much less write about something so personal and devastating. And so I decided to put off writing a larger story.

In part due to the immense outpouring of interest and concern from readers, an expression of emotion for which I'll always be grateful, I wrote dispatches and updates on Amelia's progress for the *Review-Journal*. Those stories are collected in this book.

While our doctors and therapists help us write the happy ending to Amelia's long journey, I am proud to offer this small, spirited volume with partial sales proceeds to benefit several children's cancer charities.

This book's publication was made possible by *Review-Journal* publisher Sherman Frederick, editor Thomas Mitchell, Stephens Press publisher Carolyn Hayes Uber, manuscript editor Jami Carpenter, book designer Sue Campbell, production coordinater Stacey Fott, and newspaper librarians Padmini Pai and

Pamela Busse. Thanks also to Jim Laurie and Kelsey Laurie.

Amelia at the time of her brain tumor diagnosis.

Introduction

When our eight-year-old daughter Amelia was diagnosed with cancer in October 2004, my wife Tricia and I were nearly overwhelmed by fear for the life of our only child. After enduring years of misdiagnoses for her daily nausea and fierce headaches, the proper medical call was finally made on a miserable, overcast October afternoon. The awful challenge was whether she would live long enough for the truth of her brain cancer condition to matter. A malignant, mixed-cell tumor was located in the middle of her brain, and emergency surgery was ordered. She had just hours to live.

Her survival and recovery from the brain surgery was only the beginning of a long battle against cancer and all that goes with it.

Amelia's long journey has been aided by family, friends, nurses, therapists, and lots of doctors.

As a columnist for the *Las Vegas Review-Journal*, I spent weeks weighing whether or not to write about her experience. I finally decided that no story I would ever cover would be more important than the one that was playing out in front of me. The deadline-driven columns contained in these pages were written for the newspaper in the difficult months that followed her diagnosis.

Today, Amelia is a beautiful thirteen-year-old with a wide circle of family and friends who love and cherish her. She attends Cadwallader Middle School, studies piano, competes in wheelchair sports, and works hard to squeeze the most out of life each day. She loves to cook and play Scrabble with her mom and swim and tend her herb garden with her dad. And she's making the transition to life with a wheelchair without complaint. Her grace under life's greatest challenges has awed her parents and inspired her community.

There is no greater honor than having her as a daughter.

— John L. Smith

Part I: The Sunny Days Before

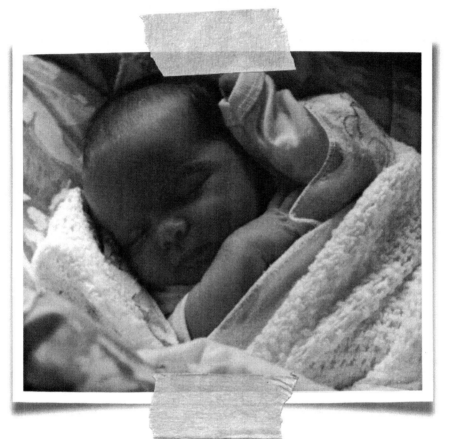

A bundle of pure sunshine.

February 2, 1997

A great day arrives for Amelia's proud parents.

If you didn't know better, you might think it was just another day in Family Court.

The half-bored bailiff senses something in the air, something like spring. A trip to Family Court does not normally generate smiles and salutations. But today is different. The bailiff greets my wife, Tricia, and me with a grin and can't help smiling at our Amelia wrapped in my arms. Everyone loves my little girl. She is a sweet, twenty-pound bundle of pure sunshine.

Today, Amelia becomes ours forever.

Today, a judge will decide that our ten-month-old adopted daughter is officially and irrevocably ours. Ours in name, ours in law. Ours like the moon and stars.

She had been ours in spirit from the moment we met her birth mother, a bright, beautiful young woman who immediately knew we were the right people to care for the life she accidentally had made. But when it comes to adoption, ten months is like one hundred years. A lot can happen, and most of it's bad.

What others could not know was the agonizing longing childless couples go through as they travel through the years hearing the voices of other people's children. Others could not appreciate the surgeries Tricia had endured and the painful questions that remain unanswered when couples fail to produce offspring.

We knew we were taking a chance when we decided to adopt, but no one enters into the process without feeling a fair amount of desperation. The potential was nothing compared to the prospect of a gray life without a child. I know plenty of couples who are delighted not to have kids, and that's good for them, but some people are meant to have children.

In late November we sat in Judge Steve Jones' courtroom and listened as two dozen couples were divorced in rapid succession. Families were dissolved in an instant, and Tricia and I held hands and were awed by the awful matter-of-factness of it all.

Then it was our turn. We had come to have the rights of the biological parents terminated and entered the courtroom fretting over everything that might go wrong. Instead, everything went right. The judge looked only a little puzzled when the couple sitting before him began crying like children.

Then we waited until our attorney, John Hunt, decided it was time to move forward. Our state caseworker, Barbara Draper, had finished her background check, and we counted the hours while we raised the baby in our home.

Today is the day.

We arrive early for court. We remember the baby, but forget the cameras we set aside at home to capture this moment. As if in a thousand years we might forget.

Other couples are there. We share smiles and nods of understanding, but we keep to ourselves. So close to our goal, no one is too confident. It is as if we might accidentally break the delicate bond that tethers us to our children.

Amelia has smiles for everyone. And a message for me.

"Dada," she says, resting in my arms. "Dada, dada, dada."

It is the greatest word I've ever heard. Now it's time to see the judge.

In his chambers, Judge Gary Redmon calmly greets us. Recalling those divorce actions and all the calls I've received from parents clawing and scratching for possession of their children, I do not envy the judge his job. At Family Court, this is one of the few instances in which a judge makes a decision guaranteed to please everyone in the room.

The adoption process, a culmination of months of hoping for the best and worrying about the worst, is over in a few moments. The judge congratulates us, smiles at Amelia, and comments on how beautiful she is. We beam as proud parents will.

Through eyes blurry with tears, I make out the part of the document that reads, "Now, therefore, it is ordered, adjudged and decreed that the said minor child is hereby declared to be adopted by Petitioners, Patricia Smith and John L. Smith, that said minor child shall henceforth be regarded and treated as Petitioner's natural child and have all the lawful rights as their own child, including the rights of support, protection, and inheritance . . ."

I hold the adoption decree like a deed to the future itself. Years of anguish melt away in the warmth of this moment. Amelia is ours for good, ours forever, ours like the moon and stars.

"Mama," our girl says, reaching out her small hand to touch Tricia's cheek.

"Yes," my wife says, her eyes wet with joy. "It's me, mama."

All Pooh fans raise your right hand.

Charismatic bear holds one big part of a little girl's heart

It started in the middle of the night with a sharp stabbing pain in my ribs. I rolled over, awoke with an anguished cry in the dark.

Cardiac? Gall bladder? Bad tuna casserole? Nothing so tame.

It was Piglet. Hard plastic and sharp as a Ninja throwing star. One of the bear's buddies. We're talking Pooh, Winnie T.

I took it as a sign, uttered something unprintable, and hurled the offending swine into the night. Piglet landed ears up. I know this because I stepped on it on the way to the bathroom. It was then my wife, Tricia, and I realized that our sweet, wonderful, priceless daughter, Amelia, had been abducted by the worldwide Pooh Cult.

Forget Scientology. This Pooh guy is everywhere. With chapters in every store in America, he's the Reverend Sun Yung Pooh.

He is such a tubby-little-chubby-all-stuffed-with-fluff type of fellow that he's sure to deceive casual observers. "Bear of very little brain," indeed. He fooled me at first, but no more.

Pooh crept into my daughter's life subtly, the way they all do, the little masher. First it was a harmless stuffed Pooh with a musical honey pot. Kind of sweet, you know? Then it was the official Pooh cup, spoon, and bowl set. And the Pooh bib, of course. Those I could live with.

But add to that the Poohjamas, bed sheets, and Pooh house with wicked plastic friends (batteries not included), and even I began to spot a pattern. Our little girl was showing the early signs of addiction: All Pooh, all the time.

"The first step is to admit you are powerless to control this Pooh," I told Amelia.

"Oh, brother," her eyes replied.

"It's a phase," my wife said. "She'll grow out of it."

I said, "I don't know. It's Pooh today, head-banging rock music tomorrow. By the end of the week she'll want credit cards and the keys to the Sentra."

For us the turning point came when we made the mistake of letting her watch the cult's indoctrination video, "Winnie the Pooh and the Honey Tree."

"Harmless viewing," family members said. "She'll love it."

One sitting and our little girl was lost to us. At least temporarily. She stared transfixed, hanging on every syllable and song. When the end credits appeared on the screen, she began to chant, "Pooh, Pooh, Pooh." This Pooh is her Mick Jagger, her Sandy Koufax, her Mahatma Gandhi.

My wife and I stared at each other, baffled by the silly seduction that takes place time after time in the Hundred-Acre Wood. Amelia only became more enamored with each viewing.

"Pooh, Pooh, Pooh," she cried. "Pooh, Pooh, Pooh."

In our home, we dare not speak the name. One rhetorical misstep and her mantra echoes through the house. She halts her freestyle Crayola wall mural, which I must say shows genuine artistic promise, and marches like a midget zombie toward the television.

"Pooh, Pooh, Pooh," she calls.

Papa? He's passé. Mama? A mere memory. Pooh has taken control.

Our happy family.

So for us it's icksnay on the oopay. We have developed code words for Mr. You Know Who. He is "The Bear," "Ursa Cartoonae," and the "Tubby Little Cubby Pain in the Patoot."

Recently the Pooh problem grew acute when my wife brought home a potty chair.

Now, Amelia is an apprentice potty trainer with real potential. Her trouble is semantical, I suspect. After all, when we say "poo," she hears "Pooh," and immediately goes into a trance that would impress the Mummy.

Her mantra never wavers: "Pooh, Pooh, Pooh."

"No, honey," I said. "Not Pooh. Poo. Put poo in the toilet."

Amelia looked askance, shrugged, and ambled across the room. She returned a minute later with her stuffed Winnie under one arm, grinning at me, and jammed the willy-nilly silly old bear head-first into the potty.

That's my girl.

When I tuck her in at night, struck silent
by her sweet perfection, I know I am a father
of very little brain who frets over the smallest
things. The twinge I feel is her presence in my
heart. I say a prayer for her, for our family.

My wife and I spent years hoping for a child.
Now that we have Amelia, we must prepare,
day by day, to give her back to the world. That
thought humbles me, and I am overwhelmed
by the assignment. But I know it's better to
just live and do your best than sweat the
possibilities.

Eventually, I know this Pooh thing will pass.
To be honest, it's that subversive Barney who
really has me worried.

It's a hat party.

Daughter's sunshiny smiles make
Father's Day a formality

I stand in the doorway after a day bad enough to depress Dostoyevsky, feeling lower than the welcome mat I'm standing on, and then I see her.

Two feet high with a head full of blond curls, she hears the door open and takes off like a runaway pony across the living room. She calls my name, and I swear I am ten years younger and nothing on earth matters more than this moment.

She throws her arms around my knees and nearly knocks me to the floor, for I have become feather-light and dizzy. I am a palooka of putty in her hands. I hug her tight, smell her hair like hyacinth, hear her giggle at my tickle, and am warmed by her smile. The soundtrack to this reverie never varies.

"You are my sunshine, my only sunshine," I hear as the bad day melts away.

Right now I am not the half-wit wordsmith, but the king of the whole wonderful world. I have won the lottery and an Olympic gold medal, the Triple Crown, and the World Series. All we lack is confetti for our ticker-tape parade for two.

Daughter Amelia, you are my sunshine, my heart's needle, my Emmy, Oscar, and Nobel Prize.

Until she came along, Father's Day was something my dad enjoyed. But now I have learned his secret: Every day is Father's Day when your daughter smiles at you.

It's funny, really, but I didn't know what I was missing all these years. I go along, stumbling through life, thinking I'm doing something important. Then she came along.

Now she's two. Terribly, wonderfully, irrepressibly two. Her mother and I can't remember how we got along without her. Or, frankly, what a quiet, debris-free meal at home felt like.

It wouldn't be supper without a cherry tomato bounding across the dinner table like a ball through the infield. I make a backhand stab, flip to Mom's napkin and complete the double play. Occasionally, a morsel reaches the floor, where Sparky gobbles it up like a canine Ozzie Smith.

But that's my girl. In a league of her own.

Nothing is the same since she joined the team. Not meals, not sleep, not the furniture or the wardrobe.

Every shirt I own is stained. Fortunately, I'm a journalist so no one notices. I wear each mark the way a general wears his medals. Swinging in the park is fun again. Digging in the sand is an adventure rivaling anything involving Indiana Jones. A few scoops and we have created mountains and kingdoms and socks full of grit.

Lying on our backs gawking at the clouds, I can feel myself attached to the planet. And I know why.

The reason fidgets next to me like a tangle of kittens and string. She is Einstein's theory personified: Energy equals Amelia.

As if to illustrate the point, she gathers her footing and takes off giggling across the grass. Her laughter is a song and the daylight dances in her hair.

"You are my sunshine, my only sunshine . . ."

At home, Amelia helps her mother in the kitchen like a whirlwind assists a pile of leaves. It takes an hour to recover, but Mom, who does so much work and gets so little credit, never complains. Not even when she discovers days-old cookie dough and enough crackers to feed all the birds in town wedged into the couch cushions.

Yard work is the best it's ever been now that she's my assistant. She's pulled the heads off the tulips and given the bouquet to mom. It's all right. I say tulips are overrated. They'll return next year. Watering is a celebration, the Mardi Gras with a garden hose. Occasionally, the grass gets wet. The purple perennials get drunk as sailors as a sea washes over them. She saves the best dousing for herself. When I'm not looking, she drenches herself and laughs at my expression as the water fills her shoes.

My daughter is 100 percent: In all our time together, she's never missed a puddle.

My father once told me that his children and his wife were his joys in life. At the end of the day, he said, they were all that mattered. Smug as a vicar, I nodded my head but had no clue as to what he was saying.

Now I do.

So forget the bad ties. Forget the barbecue gadgets, power tools, and greeting cards. For Father's Day, I don't want tickets to the ballgame or a bottle of scotch. The greatest gift a man could ever receive greets me at the door each night with a hug strong enough to make the world a better place and a laugh that makes time stand still.

She is my sunshine, sweet Amelia. Every day is Father's Day now that I have her.

"I'm a schoolgirl now."

September 2, 2001

Parents survive child's first day of school

Toss and turn and try to rest, but the electricity that hums in the late-night air makes sleep impossible. It's two a.m., officially the first day of school.

The bell announcing the commencement of kindergarten is a mere six hours, fifty-five minutes away, but the excitement and tension have become too great.

Not for our five-year-old angel, who sleeps heavily beneath a butterfly mobile in her bedroom, but for her jittery parents, who stare like deer into the headlights of time wondering where the years have gone.

Was it just yesterday we bundled her up and brought her home from the hospital, so awed by the moment that we dared not speak for fear of breaking the spell?

In a million years I never could forget the hum of that quiet car as my wife and I chauffeured our sweet, pink dream-come-true through the city streets. It's a hum I hear again this morning, the unmistakable murmur of time passing, the whisper of life reminding us that the days are but leaves on the breeze. Fluttering, fleeting.

Kindergarten: A German word meaning, "You didn't think she would stay small forever, did you?"

Well, yes. I did. I lived quite comfortably in denial.

But there's no denying this big day when our dear daughter passes into a new world not entirely defined by Mom and Dad. She's been buzzing about this day for weeks as she pored over her new school clothes, trying on one outfit after another and carrying on dramatic imaginary dialogues with her new friends and teacher. She finally decided on a splendid blue dress with shiny red shoes. A smart selection, I say.

Her little backpack is empty, and Mom and I fight the impulse to load it with hearty provisions, a first-aid kit, and a lengthy list of emergency phone numbers. You know, just in case. If we had our way, she'd need a Nepalese sherpa to get to school.

I remind myself she's not trekking to Tibet for five years, just kindergarten for two-and-a-half hours, but I know the trip she's really taking is the one that leads to the future and independence.

Nothing our little family imagined has prepared us for the moment she leaves our hands to join Mrs. Starks' classroom, one filled with all the colors of the new Las Vegas. Her teacher is bilingual, her new friends come from down the street and faraway places. In a minute she seems at home.

The playground is the great equalizer, the place with no language barrier, where an aptitude on the monkey bars is highly prized. Amelia's there moments before the first bell rings, and I shoot a roll of film before reminding myself that she's not joining the Marines, just the Class of 2014.

Then the bell rings. Mom and I wince. Not yet. Just a little longer.

Amelia kisses my cheek and whispers, "I'm a schoolgirl now."

Yes, sweetheart. And my only regret is that I can't stop the clock before she skips out of our lives and into the playground of the world.

An actress at heart, in a dramatic voice that would have made Sarah Bernhardt proud, she tells Mom, "I'm just so happy I could cry," then disappears into the classroom.

I had rehearsed this moment often. I had imagined Amelia breaking down in tears and needing the kind of emotional support that only professional parents could provide. In my dream, I calm my daughter with something intelligent like, "It's okay. You're a big girl."

But she's not the one crying.

❋❋❋

Afterward, my wife and I sit at Starbucks like dazed palookas knocked punchy by the morning's meaning. We're thinking of our good fortune.

And of her uncanny ability as a baby at breakfast to place a Cheerio on the end of her nose. And of the moment she first called me Dad. And of the day she took her first step. And of her little hands in ours. And of countless other moments in our time as the luckiest parents in the world.

It's not as if we had showed promise. Before Amelia, Tricia and I turned Boston ferns brown overnight and killed more pet store finches than a score of ravenous tomcats. But kids are surprisingly durable, and ours is surviving Parenting 101. The car is quiet again as we head back home on the first day of school, the only sound, the hum of two hearts too full for words.

Part II: The Battle of A Lifetime

Fishing at Bishop, California.

November 7, 2004

A doting father's get-well message to the daughter of his dreams

I dreamed of you, Amelia, long before we first met. You were a voice laughing through cotton candy clouds as I slept as a child. Even as a boy I hoped one day to become a father, but I never imagined holding someone as perfect as you.

When Tricia and I brought you home that spring day in 1996, your sweet pink face smiled up at us from new blankets. You were our dream come true and the answer to our prayers for a family of our own. We knew we'd met an angel and felt humbled by the gift we'd received.

We named you Amelia after the famous flier. Oh, how our spirits soared.

You grew into a beautiful eight-year-old with golden curly hair that never failed to attract compliments from strangers everywhere we went. You accepted praise gracefully. The truth is that your beauty has taken my breath away from the first day I held you and bathed you in the bathroom sink.

When you complained of headaches and a tummy ache, we took you often to a pediatrician. When the headaches grew acute, we took you in one more time and thought you suffered from migraines or the flu. Thankfully, a doctor ordered an emergency MRI.

Nothing could have prepared us to hear the words "brain tumor." We were staggered but were told the tumor was likely benign.

Your mother asked for the best surgeons available, and the physicians at University Medical Center set egos aside and professionally recommended the experienced team from

Barrow Neurological Associates at St. Joseph's Hospital in Phoenix.

The UMC doctors even booked the medical flight to Arizona, and eighteen hours after your MRI, you and your mother boarded the single-engine airplane. You flew back into the clouds that October afternoon, and I was reminded of the way you had first come to me in a boy's dream. Was I dreaming still?

There was no room for Dad on the little plane, and no immediate commercial flights available, so I threw clothes into suitcases and with your Aunt Cathy sped over U.S. 93 and Hoover Dam, across the northern Sonoran desert, down U.S. 60 past miles of saguaros into the outskirts of Phoenix.

Every road construction detour was agonizing. Each stoplight was an eternity.

Your mother saw no other planes were on the ground as the emergency flight approached Sky

Harbor Airport. When she asked why, the pilot said President Bush was in town for a debate and all commercial flights were canceled. You had the sky all to yourself.

As the plane landed, your mother looked out the window and saw Air Force One gleaming in the late afternoon sun.

All the way across the dark desert, I was tormented by the thought of how much your head must have hurt and how little you complained until the pain grew so intense you couldn't help screaming. I will hear that cry the rest of my life.

I made it to your bedside that night in time to hear the surgeon tell us the tumor was in a "catastrophic" location, blocking a brain ventricle and the flow of your spinal fluid. If everyone hadn't acted so quickly, we would have lost you.

The walnut-sized tumor had to be removed immediately, neurosurgeon Kris A. Smith told us. The mass was not benign as first believed, but malignant, a mixed-cell cancer that threatened the brain and spinal cord.

Less than a day after you landed in Phoenix, they wheeled you into surgery. Despite assurances from a team of experienced surgeons, as the operating room doors closed we still wondered whether we'd ever see you again.

The smile on the face of Dr. Smith, a fourth-generation Nevadan with family roots in Yerington, let us breathe again. After five hours, you were recovering in the pediatric Intensive Care Unit and telling us that your awful headache was gone. The eight-inch surgical incision is obscured by your golden hair, and the team of doctors is optimistic that, with aggressive chemotherapy and radiation, you will be cured.

We don't look forward to winter, but hope that by spring we'll be celebrating your full recovery

and watching this terrible time fade like a
distant dream.

The "Amelia" sign with Kelsey and Janet.

November 9, 2004

Getting by with a little help from our friends

The Kyle Canyon aspen turned ahead of
schedule this year, and most of our neighbors in
Old Town anticipated an early winter.

I thought of that as we drove up state Route
157 just after sunset, returning home for a
short time while Amelia recovered from brain
tumor surgery and prepared, as much as an
eight-year-old is capable, for a long winter of
chemotherapy and radiation.

Then we saw them.

As the headlights illuminated the narrow
street ahead, we saw that the trees once again
were yellow. Not with leaves this time, but with
ribbons. The ribbons hung from the aspen, were

tied around the pines. Even a few power poles were dressed in yellow bow ties.

As we reached the turn near the elementary school where our daughter attends third grade, A-M-E-L-I-A was spelled out in little yellow ribbons tied to the chain-link fence by her classmates. Our yard bloomed with ribbons. On our front porch was a neatly wrapped Sunday dinner still warm from the oven, courtesy of neighbors Patty and Richard.

It was the start of a week of rest and recuperation, and the beginning of a realization that we weren't facing our fight alone. Our families had always stood by us, and a few longtime friends stepped up at a crucial time to care for everything from the dogs and hamsters to flat tires and home security.

Our neighbors organized dinners and volunteered their time. We were touched by their caring concern.

Co-workers at the *Review-Journal* were very kind, and the folks at my second job at KVBC-TV, Channel 3, volunteered for service beyond the call of duty.

Gambler Lem Banker placed a bet for Amelia, and the gang at the Tap House and Fellini's sent her a portable DVD player so she could watch her favorite movies during medical treatments. Even former President Jimmy Carter sent Amelia a letter of support.

Amelia now has enough stuffed animals and balloons to open her own toy store. True to her nature, she's already begun giving away her overstock to "the sad kids who don't have any" around the pediatric unit. That's our girl.

Although private people when it comes to questions of religious beliefs, we've thrown open our psychic doors and are gratefully accepting all positive energy. This is no time for splitting spiritual hairs.

Ours is now your basic Catholic, Jewish, Lutheran, Mormon, evangelical Christian, and Buddhist extended family. We're collecting prayers, chants, and good karma. Even the chairman of the Hopi, Wayne Taylor Jr., invited us to visit his nation, where the spirits sing on the desert breezes.

What our sweet friend Rose Meranto calls "good vibes" flows our way. And not to be outdone, our atheist friends call often with warm wishes and the latest news from the rapidly changing medical front.

We've received more kindnesses than one hundred columns could recount, but, most of all, we were awed by the strength of our friends, Bruce and Theresa Monzulla, who came to our house to tell us to be aggressive and never stop fighting. The time is worth all the effort, they said.

Not once did they mention that their beautiful daughter had lost her courageous fight with a brain tumor. They didn't have to. They'll wear that agony in their eyes the rest of their lives. For us they set aside their own pain to encourage us and give us hope.

And there was Jerry DeSimone, who called to remind us that he and his wife, Sheila, recently sent their daughter off to college after her successful fight against Hodgkin's disease.

Our rest time lasted just long enough to remind us there were more people than we might have imagined rooting for our little girl's recovery. We would have rather stayed and slept right through the winter, but we had some unavoidable medical business to attend to back in Phoenix.

As we drove back across the desert, a yellow ribbon tied to my wife's car danced in the wind. From a distance it resembled a child's golden hair, an exotic bird flapping its wings, or a flickering image of hope itself.

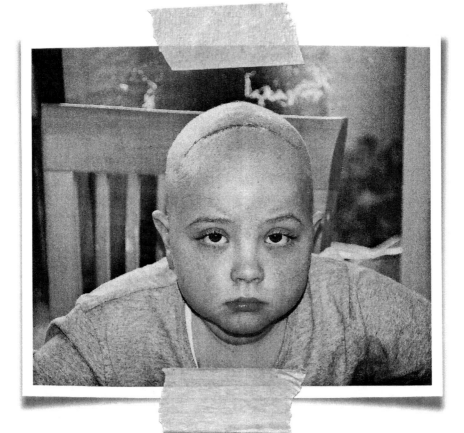

After a tiring round of chemotherapy.

November 24, 2004

Daughter's struggle against cancer provides lesson in being thankful

This Thanksgiving I find myself more thankful than at any time in my life.

We are in the middle of what many people would call a horrible experience, Amelia's medical treatment for a cancerous brain tumor.

"Thankful?" you ask. "For a brain tumor?"

It's awful, of course. It's painful and frightening, and I would give anything for it not to have happened. But you can't turn back the clock or become mired in the unthinkable possibilities the future might bring. The present is all we have, and so that is where we're focused. I'm thankful for that lesson.

There is pain, but there is also something incredible going on. I've been given an opportunity to be part of the life of a brave little girl who just happens to be my daughter. I'm awed by this opportunity — even though what I've seen has sometimes been almost too much to bear.

Pushing a chemotherapy stand behind her the other day, I watched Amelia stoop as she took the slow, painful steps of an old woman. At that moment, she might have been one hundred. Her back ached from a spinal tap, her chest hurt from a surgically implanted medical port, and I ached along with her. But I was awed by her strength.

It was then I made sure to remind myself to be thankful — thankful because a battery of tests came up negative for the spread of cancer from her brain to her spine, thankful because that medical port would nearly end the need for all the painful needles in her arms, hands, and neck. Thankful because she was winning a fight other children in the pediatric ward of St. Joseph's Hospital in Phoenix were losing.

Two days later, Amelia was energetic enough to walk to the pediatric playroom, where the kids congregate whenever possible to play games, practice arts and crafts, and visit with people more their own size and age.

I was thankful that she was walking at all, for the little boy we'd met earlier in the day had been born with spina bifida and would be wheelchair-bound all his life. His parents had stood by him through dozens of surgeries. Although he was just a small boy, he'd been using his wheelchair for so long that his tiny hands were knots of muscle. That young kid was tougher than most of the professional athletes I've met.

Amelia and the boy had had minor surgeries on the same morning, and they had that in common — that, and an affinity for Sponge Bob — and became instant friends.

Later, when the effects of her chemotherapy treatment made her quiet, lethargic, and queasy, I saw the color drain from her face and felt my heart sink. But she has improved steadily, and the doctors and nurses smile when they see her. Neurosurgeons and oncologists love a success story in the making.

This process is teaching us that not all angels play harps and float on clouds. Plenty of them work twelve-hour shifts disguised as pediatric nurses.

It's great that our nurses are professionals, some who specialize in caring for chemo kids, but their kindness is what makes them so remarkable. They don't have to share their supper, handcraft a little girl a pair of earrings, dress her in hospital scrubs like a miniature doctor, or invite her horseback riding as an incentive for getting well soon, but they've done that and a hundred other things.

Only a fool wouldn't be thankful.

These days, Amelia loses her beautiful golden strands with every brush stroke, but I am thankful because I know her hair will grow back one day. One day, when her chemotherapy and radiation treatments are finally over. One day, when the memories of all the needle sticks and morning booster shots and nauseating medicine are a thing of the past.

One day, when she's well again.

Just a few years ago a malignant tumor in such a precarious place in the brain might have been inoperable, or at best caused irreparable damage during surgery. As unfortunate as we might sometimes want to feel, we're incredibly blessed to be living in an age of medical possibilities. Slowly, a painful step at a time, she's getting better.

How could I be anything but thankful for that?

Amelia and her dad share hair care secrets.

December 5, 2004

Anything to see her smile

When we told Amelia that chemotherapy would make her beautiful curly hair fall out, she nodded and accepted the fact. She was quiet for a moment.

"All my friends love me, so it will be okay," Amelia said, doing what she always does, making the best of the bad, taking the most from the least.

She took the news far better than her mom and dad, who have proudly accepted scores of compliments about those lovely blond locks for most of our daughter's eight years of life.

After emergency surgery in mid-October to remove a malignant brain tumor, she entered a world of doctors and nurses, needles and MRIs, pain and isolation, and the presence of many very sick children. As much as we want to take away her pain, the best we can do is stand by her side and comfort her whenever possible.

Truth is, I've been a fool for Amelia since the day Tricia and I brought her home. My daughter has endured my best Henny Youngman routine every day of her life. I live to make her laugh, ache to see her smile.

I was thinking of that when I told her, "If you want, Dad will cut off his hair so we can be the same."

She had been having a down day and shrugged. She said she didn't think so. I said nothing but was secretly relieved. I've never had a crush on Kojak.

After a moment, a sparkle came to her green eyes as she focused on my head and weighed the possibilities. Then she flashed her little girl grin.

"Well, maybe," she said.

A few days later, just as the doctors had promised, her hair began falling out. She and her mother brushed it and arranged it, sprayed it and used all manner of clips, but there was no turning the tide.

When Michael from Hair In Motion finished the job with electric clippers, Amelia's long surgical scar was clearly visible, but overall she was relieved not to have to worry about her hair anymore. By then I began to believe that she'd forgotten about my promise.

On the contrary, major brain surgery had done nothing to diminish her prodigious child's memory. She voted for follicle defoliation. That's how I found myself at The Barbers in downtown Phoenix requesting the "King and I" special.

Dad's buzz cut was kind of scary.

I tried to take solace in the million-to-one shot I might look like one of those popular hip-hop rappers or at least Kojak. Bill Klaes, a barber with forty years' experience, grabbed his clippers and said the process would be over before I knew it.

"It's not real difficult to get this one to taper in and to blend in," he said, chuckling as the clippers buzzed away.

The job was finished in the time it takes to boil an egg. A large, weird egg.

"I'm really impressed with how that looks," the barber said.

I noted that he wore glasses and reminded him of that fact.

"Oh, I can see fine at a distance," he said. Which, frankly, is not the first thing I look for in a barber.

He held up a mirror. I wasn't groovin'. I was Gollum. Visions of being mistaken for E.T. or

Billy Bob Thornton in Sling Blade danced in my hairless head.

I wasn't hip-hop happenin'. I wasn't Kojak cool. I wasn't Yul Brynner, or even Mr. Clean. I was the world's largest Chia Pet.

The moment of truth came when I returned to St. Joseph's Hospital, where Amelia was having an okay day. She immediately smiled.

"You did it," she said.

"Of course," I replied.

She and her mom had read brochures on wigs and wig hats and floated a few of the options. Each was rejected. Amelia didn't want someone else's hair on her head. She wanted her own. We even considered taking her ponytail and turning it into a hair extension but rejected that, too. Instead, her mom found her a cool blue beret.

And I noticed that for the first time since her hair loss that she left her bed and strolled the hall without wearing her beret, showing passers-by and the kids in the pediatric playroom not only her baldness, but that wicked scar as well. She was more comfortable with herself, and that was the whole point of the exercise.

In the playroom, Amelia couldn't wait to attend the going home party for one little girl, who had finished her last chemo treatment and celebrated with cupcakes. With her wisps of black hair returning, her shiny gold earrings gleaming, that little girl beamed from the attention.

Amelia still has a long way to go, but we're looking forward to a cupcake party of our own one day.

Meanwhile, she'll keep making the best of the bad, taking the most from the least. Her mother will keep the faith, and I'll keep playing the clown.

Anything to see her smile.

With Mom on Christmas morning.

December 24, 2004

Brave girl emboldened in cancer fight knowing Santa's on her side, too

We drove to a Phoenix mall under the guise of gift shopping, but what we were really looking for was a little Christmas spirit and a few words with Santa Claus.

Amelia was between chemotherapy treatments, and the daily Neupogen shots administered by Tricia had kept her white cells strong. We had been so busy focusing on our eight-year-old's recovery that it left us with little time to consider something that was on her mind.

Not the brain tumor surgery. Not the chemotherapy or impending radiation treatment. Not even the other sick kids in the St. Joseph's

Hospital pediatric ward. What Amelia really wanted to know was whether Santa came to malls in Phoenix, and whether she would be out of the hospital in time to see him and put in her request.

Now, you're probably thinking that by age eight many kids have stopped believing in Santa. That's sad but true. These days, thanks to the all-pervasive adult nature of pop culture, some young people get the kid squeezed right out of them by the time they're in kindergarten. When little girls are encouraged to dress like Britney Spears or some other pop tramp du jour, there isn't much room left for childhood. And the Santa ritual is all about childhood.

Amelia at times has been skeptical, what with the world being so big and sleighs being so small. She's also had a fair number of classmates recount the twisted and terribly inaccurate tale of how Santa isn't real, but just something parents tell their kids to keep them in line until the end of the year. If Santa came in June, kids could feel justified messing off the remaining six months. But with Santa conveniently arriving at Christmas, they have that big S hanging over their heads the whole year.

There have been moments Amelia showed the ratiocinative reasoning of Lt. Colombo as she interrogated her parents about the minutest details of the Santa story. For Tricia and me, the tension was palpable. Even the slightest wavering in our explanation would nail us, and we'd be crapped out at Christmas. She'd sweated us pretty good, but we stuck to our story.

Then Amelia got sick and life got complicated. Her surgery and treatment consumed us, but we knew we couldn't let this trouble run our lives. That's how we wound up wandering around the mall in search of presents and a little Christmas spirit.

We picked up a few things and stopped at the Dippin' Dots concession. Amelia laughed at the strange face I made at the sight of the bowl of tiny ice cream pellets that looked more like bits of styrofoam than her new favorite flavor, chocolate chip cookie dough.

While her mom was shopping in secret, we walked through the mall, Amelia's baldness concealed beneath a blue beret. We talked about one of our favorite movies, *Mulan*, the story of the Chinese girl who defies tradition, cuts her hair, goes to war in her father's place, and saves her country. She was very brave, that Mulan. I know a girl just as brave, I tell her.

Amelia sings a lyric from the movie, "When will my reflection show who I am inside?"

I tell her my favorite line, "The greatest gift and honor is having you for a daughter."

Then it was time for Santa. We'd been to the mall a couple times and had missed the big guy, but this time we were in luck. Not only was he in, but the line was short. Usually Amelia and Santa have their picture taken together and share a few confidential moments. This year, her parents crowded into the photo as she whispered her request.

"What did you ask Santa for Christmas?" Tricia said later.

"I asked him to have my treatments go well," Amelia said.

"What a coincidence," I said. "That's what Mom and Dad want for Christmas, too."

She's back in the hospital now, finishing a chemo treatment. She endures all the ugly side effects with few complaints and is happiest when she can wheel down to the playroom for the chance to make a craft or talk to someone her own age. At night, the pin-sized lights on the little Christmas tree in her hospital room flash red, green, blue and yellow.

Thanks to Amelia, we found our Christmas spirit.

Dr. Steve Abella was one of Amelia's favorite.

Ordinary trip to restaurant, an extraordinary treasure

Every morning is a small miracle, each day a blessing in its own way. Each night offers the chance to dance to the music that's played. The hardest part is learning to listen.

I've been thinking a lot about such things in recent months as I've watched Amelia bravely face brain tumor surgery and the awful effects of aggressive chemotherapy. Week after week she's gamely fought to get better — and she's getting better.

We've been bolstered by optimistic news from our doctors and heaping amounts of thoughts, prayers, and gifts from our family and friends.

There have been hard days, but there also have been good days. There's happiness in living in the moment and beauty in ordinary things.

I was reminded of that the other night as we entered the enormous Phoenix cowboy steakhouse called Rustler's Rooste, which clings to South Mountain and looks out on a valley that annually challenges Southern Nevada in the nation's fastest-growing-community category.

Rustler's Rooste is one of those understated places that seats 1,500 and features a wild west theme, indoor waterfall, slide from the bar to the dining room, a country band nightly, and rattlesnake on the menu.

Amelia had heard about it from somewhere in the St. Joseph's Hospital pediatric underground and couldn't wait to go once she was out of the hospital.

Her oncologists, Hardeo Panchoosingh and Steve Abella, had told us most chemo kids experience fatigue and neutropenia — a blood disorder that reduces the body's ability to fight infection — from the chemical bombardment of her body, but Amelia bounced back rapidly from the five-day, in-patient treatments. We felt incredibly fortunate.

It was the night before she was to return for her final five-day session that we entered Rustler's Rooste and slid down to our table amid the sort of commotion usually reserved for rodeos and rock concerts. Amelia wore a small skullcap to cover her baldness, and she quickly took her place with the other kids waiting to use the slide.

It was one of the few times in weeks she'd had an opportunity to play with children her age. For Amelia, one of the hardest parts of this ordeal hasn't been the constant sticks of needles and daily booster shots, or even the wicked nausea that sweeps in so suddenly during chemo, but the lack of healthy kids to play with.

We've gone from beyond paranoid about germs to accepting of the fact she has to have a little fun when she can — even if it's in the middle of a chaotic cowboy steakhouse.

When the Peso Dollar Band switched to a slow number, I asked my daughter to dance. The floor was nearly empty, and an empty dance floor can intimidate the toughest cowboys and cowgirls, but she took one look at the Texas waltzers in their hats and Wranglers and just grinned.

She whispered that she didn't know how to dance like that, and I told her that was all right. I didn't either. We made a perfect team. We took turns leading and following and moving clockwise and then counterclockwise. When her mom joined us for the slow song, we three swayed to the music.

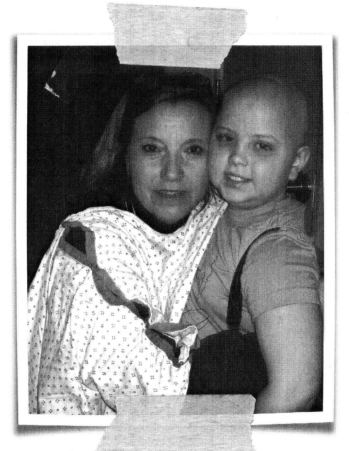

All the cancer nurses loved Amelia.

The next morning, we were back in the hospital counting down the final week of chemotherapy. It wasn't great, but Amelia toughed it out with an uncommon tenacity.

"I'm going to prove Dr. Panchoosingh wrong," she whispered to me as I tucked her in one night. "I'm not going to be neutropenic."

Fortunately for us, she was right.

All week she'd been threatening to request a poached egg party on her last day of chemo, but in the end she decided that root beer floats were more universally accepted. Despite their many maladies, the pediatric patients converged on the playroom to celebrate Amelia's achievement. They played games and sipped their floats, and only one threw up.

Now we're preparing for what we hope is the final phase, radiation. We've heard the stories. We've learned about the ugly odds and grim possibilities. But we're not victims. We're fighters. We're thankful for every morning miracle. We try to cherish the blessing in every day.

And when the music plays, we'll dance.

Amelia made great friends in the hospital.

April 10, 2005

With daughter in radiation's grip, Dad's countdown puts future in sight

Amelia was anxious for her radiation treatment to end. After so many strong days, our nine-year-old daughter was just about worn out. So I wrote her a list of reminders to help keep her focused. A day at a time, together our family would count off the final ten days of her treatment.

I didn't tell her that the list was as much for her frazzled mom and dad as it was for her.

We were grateful beyond measure that she was recovering from October surgery to remove a malignant brain tumor, but the truth is that the past six months had drained us. First, the emergency surgery at St. Joseph's Hospital in Phoenix, then the lengthy in-patient sessions of chemotherapy. For the past six weeks, she's managed to keep smiling through daily brain radiation treatments.

Many things kept us going: family and friends, faith in our medical professionals, a spiritual belief that we were meant to get through this ordeal. More than all that, there has been Amelia's quiet strength.

We arrived each morning just before her 7:30 treatment. She was always the youngest patient by many decades in the waiting room. She immediately charmed the nurses, radiation technicians, and especially her fellow patients.

The brain radiation process at St. Joe's bears a closer resemblance to a scene from a science-fiction movie than a traditional x-ray. Lying on her back, Amelia's head was held in place by a custom-fitted mesh mask. The enormous machine, about the size of a small car, rotated around her.

The process wasn't painful, but it was withering. By the end of her second week, Amelia was taking progressively longer naps. By the sixth week, she was sleeping up to fourteen hours a day. But she never complained. By the final days, we realized she was having an impact on the other patients.

"She's an inspiration," our new friend Joan from New Jersey said in a painfully raspy voice. Her throat was being radiated, and she was reaching the end of her treatment. "I figure, if Amelia can do it, then I can, too."

Amelia's radiation oncologist, Dr. John Kresl, knew what we were going through. His nine-year-old son, Logan, is recovering from brain tumor surgery. Logan has inspired all of Phoenix with his fundraising for brain tumor research. Amelia and Logan became instant friends.

Radiology technician Lacey Little calmed our fears, guided our daughter through the lengthy treatments, and surprised her with presents at just the right time.

By the final ten days, Amelia was extra tired. But she remained determined, and each morning she read from her countdown list just before heading out the door:

10. Amelia's road turns. Up ahead, in the distance, she sees the finish line and victory: healthy girl!
9. Some day soon, Amelia will have only memories of her time in Phoenix. Memories, and happy days ahead!
8. Was it really only six months ago we started our journey? The time has flown and Amelia has been the bravest girl we know.
7. We have learned many things in recent months. Most of all, we have learned to rely

on our family and friends for strength in difficult times.

6. It's Friday! It's a day to celebrate (with a delicious dessert). We also celebrate our place on the road to health.

5. It's Monday, the last Monday of radiation. Can you believe that one day we will miss this experience? Yeah, me neither.

4. On Tuesday, we take time to remember all the young friends we have met during our journey to health.

3. On Wednesday, let's think of all the kind nurses who have helped us along the way. When someone asks us what angels look like, we will tell them.

2. The road to health turns and the finish line is near. We're thankful to our God and grateful for the miracle of medicine.

1. On the last day of radiation, we celebrate our victory, thank our doctors and nurses, say 'good luck' to our friends who are still on their road.

Always grateful for life; always thankful for each day.

And now, a new journey begins . . .

To which Amelia added in large letters, "We're all done and we can go home NOW."

Yes, my love.

Now we can go home.

The Easter Bunny was good to Amelia and Mom.

April 24, 2005

TSA thwarts terrorist armed with a pink plastic purse and teddy bear

Last week, I was ordered to stand aside at Sky Harbor Airport in Phoenix and watch as an intrepid member of the crack Transportation Security Administration frisked my nine-year-old.

Amelia is a good reader and excels at math, but to my knowledge her third-grade curriculum hasn't included a single day of terrorist training. But, as they like to say around Washington these days, you can't be too careful.

She complied with the security matron's requests, and from the sidelines I assured her everything would be okay, but inside I seethed.

Forget for a moment that she was recovering from brain tumor surgery and we were flying to Las Vegas to my mother's hospital bedside. What infuriated me was the fact this was the second time in as many flights that the TSA's gumball brain trust had singled out Amelia for such treatment.

On a previous flight, my wife also was frisked. That time, the security expert's metal detector was set off by something on Amelia that seemed terribly suspicious.

"What's that?" the TSA ace asked.

Was it a bomb strapped to the body of a child who'd undergone major surgery? Those terrorists will stop at nothing to impede our freedom.

No, it was the metal chest catheter she'd had surgically implanted to help facilitate blood draws and chemotherapy.

When my angry wife carefully — carefully, so as not to be arrested for screaming — explained the situation, the security folks were then more polite and gave Amelia a toy — after they searched her little carry-on bag for weapons of mass destruction.

Last week it was my turn to witness the little tyranny against a little person. Off came her shoes, out stretched her arms.

My favorite part was when the security queen took the bomb-detecting swab and with great ceremony emptied Amelia's pink plastic purse of its contents — Walkman with earphones, Chapstick, and small pink teddy bear — and wiped the inside of the carry-on bag. Holding the swab at arm's length with a specially designed wand, the guard walked it back to the area set aside for analyzing such things.

Curses, foiled again.

After a short delay, my daughter managed to run the TSA gantlet and continue on her way.

Oddly, I wasn't searched. It was the first time in five trips that I'd been designated as something less than a flight risk. Because in recent months I've often traveled on short notice, I initially believed it was simply the style of ticket purchase that kicked me into the suspect file.

I was wrong.

"Your name is on the watch list," the friendly Southwest representative explained, asking for my date of birth. She held my driver's license, which lists my date of birth, but I decided not to quibble and complied with her request.

On the watch list? What? The watch list for poor wardrobe choice?

It's the name, she said. It's a common name, a possible alias. If I'd used an assumed name that wasn't so common, would I have received airline approval?

The TSA began as an overreaction to the September 11, 2001, terrorist attacks and the failure to act by the FBI, CIA, and other federal agencies. There was ample information that men with ties to al-Qaida and other radical Islamic fundamentalist groups had come to the United States with a plan to commit acts of large-scale terrorism. Instead of moving decisively based on information from veteran agents, the authorities acted like bureaucracies and failed to do their jobs.

That's the big story.

This is a little one.

Now a word from the Transportation Security Administration website:

"The ultimate goal of TSA service is to create an atmosphere that aligns with our passengers' need to be secure while ensuring the freedom of movement for people. In doing so our employees will assure customer confidence and ultimately establish a standard for passenger satisfaction."

By repeatedly searching children, swabbing their purses for bombs, and squeezing their teddy bears for foreign objects? Is this the America you want?

Remember, fellow travelers, it's the petty tyrannies against the little people that make us all less free.

Part III: The Relapse

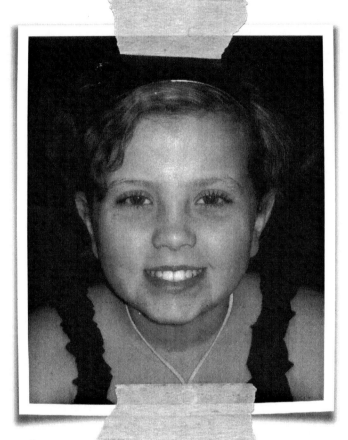

Amelia finds a reason to smile even on bad days.

Sand castle on windy beach offers shelter from waves of chaos

The Pacific Coast tsunami warning frightened away most of the tourists, and the chilly breeze blew the roller skaters off the sidewalk. It was a good day to head for higher ground, but our little beach girl Amelia was undaunted. She wanted to splash in the ocean and dig in the sand, and that was good enough for us.

Thanks to our nine-year-old's insistence, we had a small patch of Venice Beach nearly to ourselves.

There were joggers and surfers, a smattering of sunbathers, and a flock of panhandling gulls, but it wasn't nearly the sea of humanity normally seen this time of the year. Amelia was relieved to have a few hours of freedom before we returned to chemotherapy after the recent relapse of her cancer.

Following brain surgery in October at Barrow Neurological Institute in Phoenix and seven months of treatment, by early April she appeared cured of her mixed-cell germinoma. We had returned to Southern Nevada to resume our lives. Amelia had missed much of third grade, but couldn't wait to return to school.

Twenty-four hours after we came home, it was as if nothing traumatic had ever happened to her. She was amazing. She hasn't lost a step. In the first few days, she managed to appear in a school variety show and play second base for the neighborhood baseball team. We looked forward to an uncomplicated summer.

It didn't last.

A scheduled follow-up MRI revealed a new tumor, this one in her spine. A second emergency surgery was ordered, and the tumor was successfully removed. The rapid relapse meant the first chemotherapy hadn't been strong enough to stop the cancer. We faced a much harder road the second time, one that included high-dose chemotherapy, a stem cell transplant, and more radiation.

Tricia was staggered. I was angry. As usual, Amelia took the bad news better than her parents. We would trade places with her if we could, but that's not the way life works. All we could do was keep fighting.

After several chaotic days and difficult decisions, we were at Children's Hospital Los Angeles. I realized we hadn't even fully unpacked from the previous journey. I felt as bewildered as Willy Loman.

Amelia made sure we didn't forget our bathing suits. When we arrived at the beach, she yanked off her sandals and ran laughing toward the tide. Her hair is beginning to curl again and covers her surgical scar. That first operation seems like ten years ago now, but it's been only eight months.

On that afternoon in Venice, Amelia forgot about everything but the beach.

Each family has its favorite seaside activity. For some, it's lotions and books. Others like to nest beneath umbrellas and sip cool drinks. Some love volleyball, others fly kites. Many are the body surfing and boogie board types.

The Smiths dabble in several media, but our favorites are jumping waves and building sand castles. Since she was in diapers, Amelia has accompanied me into the shallow surf to laugh at the little breakers and run like scaredy cats from the big ones. Those might be our best father-daughter moments.

The castle building is a team effort. Mom, an expert cake decorator, does the sculpting. Amelia makes battlements and spectacular mountains. I mostly haul water and scoop sand. The chaos of our trip was such that we were poorly prepared for construction on our day at the beach, but Amelia improvised. Paper cups sufficed for sand scoops, and she marched down near the water line and began creating a handsome fortress decorated with smooth stones and seashells.

Her mom and dad didn't feel much like celebrating on such a windy, forbidding afternoon, but Amelia was living in the moment. And at that moment, she was happy and a million miles from the hospital, the chemotherapy, and more pain than most can imagine.

Oh, how I wanted to freeze the afternoon, to stop the day like a snapshot we could live in. But that's not possible, and before long it was time to go. We needed a good night's sleep before resuming the fight of our lives.

I made sure to drive away before the rising tide erased our castle in the sand.

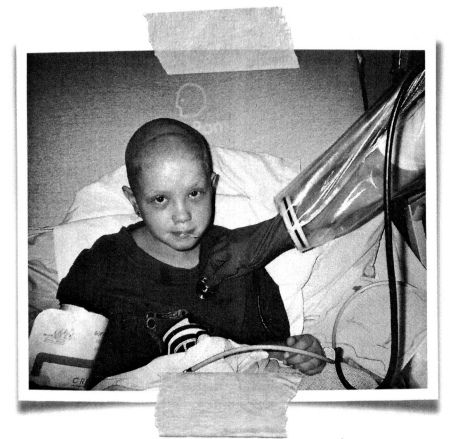

In isolation at Children's Hospital, Los Angeles.

Of the childishness of some adults and the heroics of children

I have a hard time watching sports these days. As a diehard baseball fan, that's hard to admit. After all, we go way back.

As a boy living with my grandmother at Henderson's Victory Village, I would re-enact radio broadcasts of Dodgers games. Like a flawless double play combination, Vin Scully would call the play-by-play, grandma would take his cue and relay each pitch to me in the yard through an open front door. Amazingly, the action grew more colorful thanks to her liberal scoring.

I'd take a mighty rip and circle the makeshift diamond using the mulberry trees as bases. The Dodgers were prolific home-run hitters when grandma called the game. They were even better pitchers. With Sandy Koufax or Don Drysdale on the mound, strikeouts came in clusters. Victory was certain.

It was just a kid's game, of course, but I can honestly say there was a time I was obsessed with baseball. No more.

It's not only the fact the game's steroid scandal was as overgrown as Sammy Sosa's biceps. Nor is it just the fact the players have become petulant multimillionaires with next to nothing in common with their fans. It's not even the mere fact all the multimedia coverage of the kid's game has grown so enormous there's no use even dreaming of the day the nation might put its national pastime in perspective.

By turning such issues as players' salaries and steroids into massive media dirigibles, reporters and commentators have fed a form of hero worship that's every bit as unreal as any hacked out in the golden era of the sport. Whether building up an image or tearing it down, the TV media gods create mythic figures out of .280 hitters.

As the nation prepared to tune in Tuesday's All-Star game, my wife and I sat in a room with Amelia in the oncology ward at Children's Hospital Los Angeles. I took a moment and thought of a few of the amazing kids I've been honored to meet in recent months as Amelia has gone through her treatments.

It was then I knew the old ballgame would never be the same for me. When it comes to genuine heroism, true courage in the face of pressure, and the kind of action that deserves an endless parade of praise, these kids have the players beat to pieces.

There was one boy I thought of who has battled his cancer like a Marine at Omaha Beach. Bald and frail, he was not yet thirteen. He had lost a leg at the hip and most of his energy, but there was no quit in him.

He can play on my team any day.

And there's the little boy who just turned three. When he was diagnosed with a brain tumor, his mother was forced to quit her secretarial job, move into a halfway house near the hospital, and devote every waking moment to saving the life of her son. His body had been wracked by infection and drained by chemotherapy, but he lives for the moments he's well enough to play with his plastic dinosaurs and share a simple laugh with another kid in an equally precarious place.

And there's the sweet teenage kid who had spent so much time in the hospital that some nurses could tell her stories of when she was in diapers. She was at the hospital so often her parents couldn't always make it in time for her surgery.

You want heroes, the pediatric cancer wards of this country are filled to capacity with them.

Each has a story of real grace under pressure and genuine courage in the face of some of the longest odds imaginable.

So you'll have to understand if I pass on this year's All-Star game.

These days, the real all-stars are too sick to play kids' games.

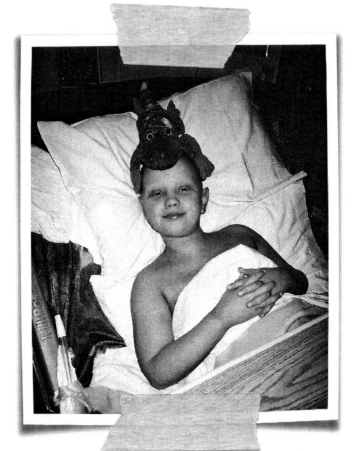

Joking with Bob the Salamander on a very hard day.

August 21, 2005

The Kid shows big leaguers the real all-star

When the Kid heard the Dodgers were coming, she made a promise to herself and her parents that she'd be ready.

Her mom and dad had been awed by her strength throughout her medical ordeal, but they didn't know how she would pull it off. So they tried to play down the visit.

They told her not to worry, that if she wasn't feeling up to it, there would be other opportunities to meet big league ballplayers. But she wouldn't think of missing her chance. Any nine-year-old who managed to play second base for her baseball team in between cancer surgeries and chemotherapy wouldn't let something like vomiting and a zero white cell count stop her.

The terrible effects of the chemotherapy had exhausted her, and, despite her fighting spirit, she was feeling awful. But the Dodgers were coming, and so she spoke the promise out loud. Promises spoken out loud mean something to the Kid. They trump simple nods, pinky swears, and written contracts signed in triplicate, everything but prayers to Jesus.

She promised she would be ready, and who were her parents to doubt her after watching her recover from two major cancer surgeries and round after round of chemotherapy? Her folks knew she'd do everything humanly possible to keep her promise. She would even cut short a chance to visit the playroom and see her new friends from the ward.

The players weren't exactly household names.

Milton Bradley, Jose Valentin, and Jeff Weaver didn't make the all-star team this year, but to the Kid and the other children in the hematology-oncology ward at Children's Hospital Los Angeles they were Hall of Famers straight from Cooperstown.

In her seven months in Phoenix, the Kid collected Diamondbacks cards and saw two games between hospital stays. Now that she was living in Los Angeles undergoing more treatment, the Angels and Dodgers had become her new favorites. A visit from an actual Dodger was almost too good to be true.

"Are they very good this year?" the mother asked.

"Not very," the father whispered. "But try not to bring it up when they get here."

The Kid didn't care if they were ten games ahead or twenty games behind. She'd be ready.

Professional athletes on the children's charity circuit travel with an entourage of publicists, television camera crews, and newspaper photographers, and the recent hospital visit was no exception. When the three Dodgers came off the elevator, the hallway was jammed with cameras.

The Kid couldn't have cared less about the media attention. In fact, the television camera made her nervous, and having strangers jam into her already crowded room was enough to make her want to pull the covers over her head.

But when Bradley came through the door in his Dodger jersey, the background chaos faded to a whisper.

He was a prince to the Kid — even though he seemed surprised by her baldness and large scar from her brain surgery. He presented her with a Dodgers cap and a gift bag of goodies, then posed for the obligatory pictures. It was probably pretty routine for him.

Some players meet sick kids out of the kindness of their hearts. Others do it to rehabilitate their public images. Still others are working off some court-ordered community service.

At one point, Bradley looked up and saw the emotion in the eyes of the Kid's parents. He must have known he'd come to the right place at the right time. And then someone mentioned the Kid's love of baseball and the fact she had gone five-for-six in a season shortened by a second cancer surgery. Only God knows when she'll get off the disabled list.

"He only gets two or three hits on a good night," a photographer cracked loud enough for everyone to hear.

The Kid beamed, that five-for-six growing as large in her mind as the Hollywood sign.

"Five-for-six," Bradley said. "You're a ballplayer."

You'd better believe it. And she knows how to play hurt.

In a few minutes, the visit was over. The Kid and the ballplayer posed for pictures, and the crowd thinned. When all was quiet again, the Kid tugged on her Dodgers cap and grinned sleepily.

Her parents knew they were gazing at the real all-star.

With our good friend and chemo nurse, Tommy.

Families in need find haven at Ronald McDonald House

If you've ever stood at a McDonald's counter, you've probably noticed a little box whispering for a donation to the Ronald McDonald House charity. Perhaps you've even slipped in some spare change. Maybe you meant to, but were too busy.

McDonald House provides a clean, safe place to stay for families of sick children. Some of the houses are relatively expansive places. Others are quite humble.

They all are populated by strangers drawn together by a single common denominator: an extremely ill child staying in a nearby hospital.

After five months at the Ronald McDonald House in Los Angeles, I've learned that this is more than enough to break down cultural and language barriers.

When Amelia was diagnosed with a mixed-cell brain tumor in October 2004, our world was instantly changed. Until that moment, we'd only thought our days in Southern Nevada were hectic. Little did we know that we were about to begin a journey that would redefine our lives.

Recent months have been dark and difficult, but we continue our fight to reach the daylight of her recovery.

It's that light of hope that I want to focus on now that we have passed the first year since her diagnosis. There was a brain surgery at Barrow Neurological Institute/ St. Joseph's Hospital in Phoenix and months of chemotherapy and radiation. Then, just three weeks after we returned home in April, a follow-up MRI showed that Amelia's cancer had relapsed, this time in her spine. After a second successful surgery at Barrow, we went to Children's Hospital Los Angeles to see Dr. Jonathan Finlay, a specialist.

To say we weren't ready for the Sunset Boulevard experience is a great understatement. The hospital was enormous, and the area apartments made us dizzy.

That's where the Ronald McDonald House comes in.

We were welcomed immediately, squeezed into an already-stuffed schedule of families all coming from somewhere else to attempt to save the lives of their children. We were able to walk to the hospital and to the supermarket from our room, and there hasn't been a day that goes by that I haven't been grateful for its location.

We were completely preoccupied with Amelia's treatment and staff members understood that. I had to thank them for the times I remembered the laundry but forgot the soap. And when our nominal weekly rent was late because we were busy pulling all-night shifts at the hospital, the staff understood.

After five months, I don't know where our family would be without the Ronald McDonald House.

We missed most of the family meetings and meals, but we slowly grew acquainted with many of the wonderful people who shared the experience with us. Though I don't recall all their names, and some I only met in passing between their own hospital marathons, I'll never forget them.

One of many images:

One warm afternoon we left the door open, and in the courtyard we heard the sounds of an electric guitar played softly. A clear, bluesy voice was singing "Sunshine on My Shoulder" by John Denver.

When I went outside to see who was making the music, I saw an enormous man with a long black ponytail sitting in an electric wheelchair, a guitar sitting across his broad chest. He tilted his head back and sang soothingly to his tiny newborn baby, who lay sleeping in a stroller in front of him.

I listened to the father coo to the daughter. I thought of all the love I have in my heart for my daughter, and how if I could sing and play, I would play my soul out for her.

Then I realized the big man was not only talented on the guitar and a loving father. He was also blind.

We still don't know where our road will lead us, but we pray every day for the strength to be up for the fight of our lives. We found an oasis amid the asphalt at the Ronald McDonald House

Los Angeles. Las Vegas also has a McDonald House that's well worthy of your generosity.

We come from everywhere. We speak many languages. We have almost nothing in common. Nothing but our children, and that was enough. The longer we travel on this road, the more we realize we really are all in this together.

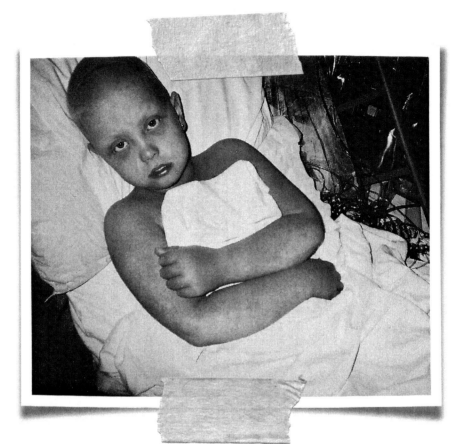

Amelia experienced many very hard days.

December 11, 2005

With child's innocence, Amelia
bestows hope and humor

It's the kind of morning full of challenges that might reduce a strong man to tears, but it's just another day in Amelia's life. About the time other kids are heading off to school, we help our nine-year-old daughter into the wheelchair that is now her constant companion. We start the day with a handful of medicine and a trip to the radiation oncologist.

It's a short drive and the actual radiation doesn't hurt, but moving from the chair to the treatment table can be agonizing for her. The waiting room is dotted with very sick patients, but none as young as Amelia. Only rarely does someone fail to comment on her smile, her inspiring attitude in the face of adversity, or her monkey-themed pajamas.

She accepts the compliments with uncommon grace, but later softly asks us for reassurance: "Am I really the bravest person you know?" Oh, yes, we tell her, the bravest ever.

Living in Phoenix in recent weeks as she's undergone the radiation we hope will stop forever the mixed-cell cancer that threatens her life, we have grown accustomed to this routine. It's one that includes radiation, physical therapy, occupational therapy, and sometimes a painful test meant to add to the growing pile of conflicting data about her medical condition.

The five months we spent in Los Angeles chasing a cure resulted in her losing the use of her legs, a condition some doctors believed was chemotherapy-related and only temporary, while others suspect it is a sign of more trouble.

It's been fourteen months since she was diagnosed with a brain tumor. In that time, we've lived in Phoenix, Los Angeles, and now Phoenix again. She has been treated by specialists with hundreds of years of combined medical experience. She's had numerous surgeries and procedures, a broad spectrum of increasingly potent chemotherapy, a stem-cell transplant, and the maximum amount of radiation possible.

She's lost the feeling in her legs, some of her hearing, her hair a half-dozen times, her fingernails, and has had her skin blistered off from chemotherapy.

But she hasn't lost hope, grace, or sense of humor.

Her parents awaken each morning with the awful feeling that even the near future is uncertain, but Amelia can't help smiling at the prospect of a trip to the zoo or the mall after her treatments are finished. It's just another day in her young life, and now she has just a week of radiation left before we finally get to go home.

Visions of Christmas and dreams of a tenth birthday in distant March fill her thoughts. She talks nonstop about the presents she wants to buy for her friends, family, and nurses. She paints an elaborate portrait of what her big birthday party will be like.

Radiation has weakened her, and we've had to postpone a few sessions while her blood counts recovered from the assault on her system, but somehow she still gets fired up by the chance to work with her physical and occupational therapists. The best part involves stretching to reach multicolored balls and tossing them at a miniature basketball rim, or playing balloon tennis. Although even a little exertion tires her, she loves the activity.

When the therapists introduce something new and take her out of her comfort zone, the anxiety is almost too much for her, but at some point in the treatment she focuses her energy and accomplishes the task.

She's learning to dress herself again, learning to get in and out of the wheelchair without being lifted. Somehow, she doesn't let the frustration and daily pain get her down.

On the contrary, Amelia's sense of humor seems to have been honed by circumstance. She laughs and jokes now more than ever. I've never known anyone her age with so many opinions — or such a willingness to express them.

She insists on wheeling herself in public, pretends not to notice the stares of strangers, graciously answers the questions of curious children who wonder aloud how she lost her hair and why she's in that chair.

Every morning she has a good reason to hide from her problems and give in to her pain, but each day she finds something to celebrate. Christmas is almost here. Radiation is almost over.

It's just another day in her life, and we know each day is a gift.

Special camps for kids with cancer helped Amelia smile again.

Hypocrites can't hijack genuine joy of giving at Christmastime

Mrs. Claus made her way through the throng of lunch-hour diners at the Meadows mall food court a couple of days before Christmas.

She smiled at shoppers, chatted with some overwhelmed moms, patted tots on the head, and warmly greeted some of the pseudo-punk teenagers, who didn't know whether to grin or be embarrassed.

I've heard a lot of nonsense lately about the hijacking of Christmas, mostly from political preachers and blowhard commentators on national television. There's not enough Christ in Christmas, they blather, and someone's to blame. There's too much crass commercialism, not enough focus on the biblical message of the holiday.

If they got any more self-righteous, I expect they'd explode.

Criticizing the commercialization of Christmas is pretty rich manure coming from TV pundits who wouldn't earn minimum wage if it weren't for the fortune in advertising dollars those commercial businesses contribute each year to media coffers. Hijack Christmas, indeed.

Besides, I like the commercial part of Christmas. Admittedly, it gets to be too much, and, yes, it would be nice to think that we'd ponder the beautiful story of Jesus a little longer before leaping into a pile of presents or tearing the stuffing out of the turkey. But it's also true that, last time I checked, there's rarely an empty seat in a house of worship for the Christmas services.

As the years pass, I find myself enjoying the bustle of the buying more and more. I love the thought of getting something for my family, of receiving the annual socks and underwear, of seeing my sweet daughter's eyes light up at the sight of enough gadgets and toys to fill a dump truck.

This is a time for contemplation, but it's also a time for celebration. It's a time for Charles Dickens and Charlie Brown, for Bing Crosby and Vince Guaraldi. I love hearing the Boss sing "Santa Claus Is Coming to Town" and will swing forever to the voices of Frank, Dino, and Tony Bennett as they celebrate the season.

Perhaps it's because my daughter hasn't been well and we consider these days precious, but the mall has become a movable feast of Christmastime excitement for our family: window-shopping, a visit with Santa, hot drinks, and plenty of laughter. Our Amelia enjoys receiving gifts, of course, but she also gets real pleasure from finding special treats for her friends and family.

Maybe that makes us hopelessly commercial, but there's genuine joy in giving. There really is magic in the season — even if all the merriment is more secular than some would prefer.

Alarmist media malarkey aside, I'm betting most kids still know the difference between Santa and the Christ side of Christmas. And if they blend the two, or you wish someone "happy holidays" because you're sensitive to the fact others just might celebrate Hanukkah or Kwanzaa — is it really a national moral crisis?

Santa isn't the Christian savior, but he's no slouch. He represents joy and giving and happiness. He brings smiles to children and a twinkle to the eyes of adults.

During a midweek stop at the Meadows mall, I saw plenty of dads with their children and heard far more laughter than lamenting. In all, people were pretty decent to each other.

That's where I encountered Dixie, also known as Mrs. Claus. Her neatly done white hair and rosy cheeks complemented her red outfit and sunny disposition. And who would have thought that after a uniform change she also doubled as one of Santa's elves?

"It's a great time of year," she said, taking a pause for the Claus. "I love this job. And I think I get more out of it than they do."

These days, I'm feeling the same way. It's been a hard year for us: Amelia's cancer treatment, the loss of my mother, and the death just last week of my wife's mom. But there's no stopping Christmas or the joy it brings to our house. (The new puppy helps — if only she would stop leaving her special deliveries on my presents.)

Throughout her radiation treatments, Amelia counted down the days with a giddiness that is music of angels to our ears. And now it's here.

So here's to Christmas, everyone, and happy holidays. No one can hijack this season, not even the hypocritical blowhards who deserve coal in their stockings.

Sonny knew a hero when he saw one.

Sonny King leaves world still smiling, and no medicine is a better cure

Peggy King was going through her late husband Sonny's personal papers the other day when she came across a letter he never got a chance to send. The great Las Vegas song-and-dance man was in the throes of cancer in 2005, and even a life force as seemingly indefatigable as his was gradually slipping.

He was in his eighties, had enjoyed a life filled with laughter and wild times in the presence of the biggest names in the music business. From twenty-eight years with Jimmy Durante to countless nights with Dean Martin, Frank Sinatra, and the rest of the Rat Pack, there wasn't anyone worth knowing from the Strip's golden age who didn't know the man born Luigi Antonio Schiavone.

Even as his condition worsened, he'd somehow managed to continue his regular weekend gigs at the Bootlegger Bistro on the Boulevard's far southern reaches. It was the spirit of the entertainer in him. But as the days wore on, he was worn out.

Despite his illness, he took time to call and ask how Amelia was doing in her own battle with cancer.

He'd read updates about her fight in my column and was among the countless people who stepped forward as fellow travelers to encourage her to never give up.

Sonny King died on February third at age eighty-three, but not before he took time to write a letter to a little girl. When Peggy found the letter recently, she sent it my way. As you

The picture of Sonny King that Amelia carries in her wallet.

might expect, she still misses her husband terribly.

"My grief for Sonny was paralyzing for quite some time," she said. "I'm able to cope a little better now. But it will be a long, long time before I'll be able to feel better."

But she also knows it was just like Sonny to set aside his life's struggle and attempt to cheer up a kid. Any kid. In this case, it was my kid.

And so I'll pass along the letter to you in hope that its simple, sincere voice encourages you in your own life struggle. If there's one thing our cancer journey has taught our family, it's that everyone has the potential to be on the road.

Dear Amelia,

I'm a friend of your dad and like many others I read his column and am following his stories about you.

Amelia, my name is Sonny King and I had chemotherapy and radiation only mine was in my neck.

Let me tell you about the survival of the sickness we both share.

First of all, you can have all the best doctors and medicine in the world, but your best doctor and medicine is the love and nearness of your mother and dad. I know you can see that love in their eyes, and no medicine is a better cure than that.

I saw the feature of you and your dad's new hairdo. He looks like a bowling ball with eyes. I looked the same way, and I wasn't ashamed because I always felt people had to like me not because of what I looked like, but because of what I am! I was very happy to read you felt the same way about yourself.

You say your dad makes you laugh, and that is the second best cure, a sense of humor. I would make jokes about my illness and people would laugh, and that would make me feel very good.

I worked for a while a very long time ago with a very big star named Jimmy Durante many, many years before you were born. His opening song is what you should always feel in your heart. It goes like this:

"You got to start each day with a song,
Even when things seem wrong."

I know you will have every success that I had with my illness, and I pray that it will happen ever so soon. I feel like I know you through your father's columns, and I want to meet you when you come home. God love you. And like the song says,

"When you're smiling,
Keep on smiling,
And the whole world smiles with you."

When I read the letter to Amelia, she nodded and said, "He's right. You have to keep smiling and never give up."

Leave it to Sonny King to bring us a smile and steal an extra bow from beyond this life.

With help from friends, she accepts every challenge.

Look on Amelia's face makes embarrassing trip to roller rink worthwhile

I wondered how Amelia would react to being invited to not one but two weekend birthday parties at the Crystal Palace Skating Center.

For that matter, I wondered how I'd react.

Left without the use of her legs after cancer surgery and chemotherapy, Amelia has now reached that age where she's begun checking her hair in the mirror and watching her mom apply lipstick. At ten, she's at an awkward in-between age that finds even children without any physical challenges less than sure-footed socially.

Chances were great she would be the only kid at the skating rink in a wheelchair, so, of course, I wanted to protect her feelings. I should have known better. She wasn't intimidated. On the contrary, she seemed uncharacteristically relaxed.

Then it hit me. Amelia had entered a world where everyone was on wheels. There were no frustrating curbs, no steps between one level and another. The floors were made for rolling.

The Crystal Palace is one of those places all kids love and most parents loathe, at least parents like me, who as a kid was enormously intimidated by the prospect of skating. Skating took coordination and skill and lots of practice, and so as a boy I immediately wrote it off as something only girls did.

When roller derby became popular, and scenes of linebacker-sized men on skates filled the back-channel airwaves, I changed my tune. But I still steered clear of the roller rinks.

Imagine Chuck E. Cheese on wheels, and you have an idea what the Crystal Palace looks like inside. With its flying skaters, flashing lights and throbbing '70s music, it's disco-meets-the-roller-derby. Such a mix makes for an ideal site for kids' birthday parties, and we spent the better parts of Saturday and Sunday celebrating the passing of cousin Janet and friend Rachel into pre-teenhood.

Amelia couldn't wait for everyone to finish putting on their skates before she headed onto the large wooden floor, her flashy front wheels sparkling as she tailed her pals in a counter-clockwise direction with occasional timeouts for "The Hokey Pokey," "Chicken Dance," and "Limbo."

She let the first-time skaters hold onto her wheelchair for balance, stopped to help a tiny kid who'd lost his mother's hand, and even led a conga line of birthday revelers snaking across the floor. What I wouldn't give to have as much confidence as my ten-year-old.

And as much skill as a lobbyist.

In short order, she began working on me to get some skates and join her on the floor. I flatly refused.

Several times, in fact. Then I caved in and felt a flood of childhood anxiety return. With one hand on her chair and the other on the wall, I started around. Tiny children zoomed past. In fact, everyone zoomed past. The embarrassment was painful. I was a hopeless Roller Dork.

Flashbacks of childhood embarrassments on the sidewalks of Henderson flipped through my brain like the pictures in a GAF View-Master. "Here's one of the Losers putting on his skates. Here's one of him whacking his head on the cement. Here's one of him crying like a baby.

Here's one of him falling down again, and again, and again."

Last weekend, I fell only once. My right wrist broke my fall, which in turn nearly broke my right wrist. The sharp pain shouted: "Hey, idiot, you're not a kid anymore" in my brain. Beached whales are returned to the ocean more easily than I regained my roller-footing.

The look on Amelia's face made the humiliation worthwhile. She couldn't stop grinning. "Good job, Dad," she said, rolling her eyes. "Thanks for trying."

I'd like to be able to tell you that when the skating lesson ended, we went to the snack bar and shared a Coke. But I could see she wanted me to get as far away from her as I could — and fast. It's bad enough getting stuck skating with your dad, but it's far worse getting trapped on the track with Roller Dork.

After the last birthday party broke up, we returned home. On the drive, the leg pains, nausea and headaches that plague her returned.

Through all her challenges, Amelia never ceases to amaze me with her grace and goodness. She reminds me to worry less and embrace life more.

My little girl is rolling to her own beat, and even the hard days are good days.

She had a great Christmas away from the hospital.

December 24, 2006

Kids with cancer show hand-wringers that Christmas is securely in place

I planned to send a season's greetings spitball to the mass media boobs who keep telling us Christmas is under attack, but I couldn't concentrate over the sound of daughter Amelia's voice as she sang along to her favorite CD by Aly and AJ.

"It's the greatest time of year, and it's here, help me celebrate it!" Amelia exclaimed, rocking out in her wheelchair. "With everybody here, friends so dear, let me simply state it: It's our favorite way to spend the holiday!"

The kid needs no microphone to communicate the message of the season. Around our house, we're grateful for every holiday we receive. Although we're Christmas-centric, the kind of people who leave their lights up past Valentine's Day, we wouldn't mind celebrating Hanukkah, Kwanzaa, or any other occasion for family and friends to gather and give thanks for the gift of life.

"Joy to the world, and everyone lift up your hearts and feel the love!" the kid sang.

Amelia wasn't thinking about the heavy sentiment, of course. She was cutting gingerbread cookie dough, belting out the high notes, and trying her best not to open a neatly wrapped present she'd just received from her friend, Kyndel Gregory.

Did I say they were friends? They surely are. Kyndel and Amelia haven't actually met yet, but they're kindred spirits. The daughter of Nancy and Gary Gregory, Kyndel was diagnosed at age sixteen months with medulloblastoma. She had her first brain surgery, later was diagnosed with a different form of cancer, and underwent a second operation followed by a series of chemotherapy and radiation treatments and tandem stem-cell transplants. The Gregorys nearly lost their daughter on more than one occasion, but today she's a healthy eight-year-old.

The Gregorys are one of many local families who have reached out to Amelia and her family over the past two years as we've endured our own battle with a brain tumor and childhood cancer. I don't know where we'd be without those families and the individuals who have shared their stories of hope and encouraged us to hang in there and fight the good fight.

With so much goodness in the world, how could anyone but a clown claim that Christmas was under attack? Now that's what I call humbug.

The kid shows her parents every day what the good life is all about.

Amelia attended two summer camps for cancer survivors: Camp Firefly at Torino Ranch and Arizona Camp Sunrise outside Payson. They're not only a ton of fun for the campers, but the gathering is a reminder that others share your experience and the circle of survivors is wide and diverse.

These days, she is e-mail pals with Lacey Butler, an exuberant teenager from Sparks whom she met at the Arizona camp. Lacey also had a brain tumor. She has lost much of her eyesight, but not her sense of humor. She should consider a career in comedy.

This past summer at camp Amelia also met Kim, who lost a leg to the disease, and Antonita, who has sickle cell. Life has dealt them mountainous challenges. They climb without complaint and show more grace in a day than the blowhards could manage in a decade.

At the risk of sounding like a character out of *A Charlie Brown Christmas*, the season isn't about all the glitz and commercialism, and it certainly isn't about all the fear-mongering, but about being grateful for life's gifts. So if you're Christmas people, sing praises to the Lord, or at least play *It's a Wonderful Life* in an endless loop until New Year's. If you're Hanukkah people, let your lights of hope and faith shine. If you celebrate Kwanzaa, shout it to the world.

That's the proper response to all the self-important media ninnies who posture and puff and question the security of the season. It's funny, really. In a way, television's self-appointed yuletide hand-wringers have become as much a part of the seasonal tradition as traffic jams at the mall and the return of long lines at Kmart.

I could go on, but I'm about to burn a batch of gingerbread cookies, and the kid hates it when I do that.

"It's the greatest time of year, and it's here, help me celebrate it," she sang. "Joy to the world! Joy to the world! Joy to the world!"

With the key to her cabin, her Make-A-Wish was granted.

December 27, 2006

A special gift delivered: volunteers build my daughter's dream

Dear Boss:

I'm not due back to work for a few days, but I wanted to tell you about something wonderful that happened to the Smiths.

When we were contacted more than a year ago by the folks at the Make-A-Wish Foundation of Southern Nevada, Amelia was interviewed and asked what she wanted from the charity, which specializes in granting the requests of children who have experienced major illness. Most kids can't wait to take their families on an all-expenses-paid trip to Disney World. For others, a dream-come-true means hanging out with a favorite movie star or pop music icon, or becoming a major leaguer or entertainment superstar for a day.

Whatever it is, Make-A-Wish tries to grant it.

But then came Amelia.

When Amelia was diagnosed with her brain tumor more than two years ago, we began an odyssey that took us from Las Vegas to Phoenix and Los Angeles. Through all the surgeries and treatment, Amelia kept one goal in mind: Get better and return home.

As the months passed, that goal manifested itself in the dream of a playhouse of her own. But not just any playhouse. She wanted something special, something with curtains and room for sleepovers.

When Amelia informed the Make-A-Wish people of her request, they must have thought she had misunderstood them. You mean, she didn't want to take the whole family to Disney World, or on a cruise?

No thanks, she said. But a playhouse would sure be nice.

Her request grew more detailed by the day. Her dream gradually morphed from Tuff Shed to Trump Tower.

You can't have a playhouse without popcorn, and for that you need a microwave. You can't have popcorn without something to wash it down, and for pop you need a mini-fridge. And on it went.

Back at Make-A-Wish headquarters, the team members must have wondered what they had gotten themselves into. But they began to network and made a connection with the Focus Property Group and its Landtek subsidiary.

Once the volunteers met Amelia, it was all over. They set out to grant her wish, which had become even more complicated by the fact that she had lost the ability to walk. Of necessity, a playhouse would have to be wheelchair accessible with a pathway from the house.

The company officials' goal was to give more than money. They wanted to give their time and attention to a charitable project, which isn't easy when everyone already has hectic working and family lives. After penciling out a plan, they got busy.

When they signed on for playhouse construction duty, they went after the assignment like Marines. As the weeks went by, they fought wind, rain, sleet, snow, and holiday pressure, but kept on working. They missed family dinners and football games, but they wouldn't quit.

On Saturday, the job done at last, Amelia cut the ribbon on her clubhouse cabin and marveled at having her wish granted so perfectly. From the curtains to the flooring, everything was ideal. There was even a microwave and a mini-fridge.

They made a brave little girl's dream come true just in time for Christmas.

It was a good day for the Smiths.

No one asked for recognition, so of course I can't resist. Alphabetically, it goes something like this: Ahern Rentals, Lenny Badger, Jack Bassett, Bob's Construction, Peter Bressler, C&C Crushing, Jeff Davis, Focus Property Group, Frazee Paint, Gothic Landscape, Steve Kevish, Landtek, Jeremy McClain, Brian Moler, John Moler, Pavestone Corp., Ted Pfisterer, Rinker Materials, The Ritter Charitable Trust, James Seebeck, Maurice C. Seebeck III, Maurice C. Seebeck Jr., Sun Valley Electric Co., Cindi Sokoloff, Michael Sokoloff, Steven Sokoloff, Team Endeavor, Becky Wildmann, and Shelly Wright.

On the wall of the playhouse, a plaque commemorates the gift and communicates the spirit of the giving with a quote from Dr. Maya Angelou. It says, "When we cast our bread upon the waters, we can presume that someone downstream whose face we will never know will benefit from our action as we who are downstream from another will profit from that grantor's gift."

Amelia says she'll even let me visit soon, as long as I promise to knock first and wipe my feet before entering her new abode.

As I write this, she's trying to figure a way to have pizza delivered to the playhouse of her dreams.

Cherishing every day.

Any problem is beatable when you've been to hell and back

It seemed everything in my life was coming apart. Though the sky was clear, I wouldn't have been surprised if I'd been struck by lightning. Perhaps you know the feeling.

In the middle of the pressure and the chaos, at a time I was being forced into personal bankruptcy, I looked up at the calendar on my desk. Suddenly, I realized no matter what hell I might endure, I would survive.

This past week was special for my family. It marked the third year since Amelia was diagnosed with a malignant brain tumor. What a journey it has been. It's a roller coaster ride I don't recommend for the faint of heart.

The trauma of nearly losing our only child is impossible to describe. It simply changes your life forever. Our lives swirled before us as we sat silently in the waiting room overwhelmed by a cascade of anxiety and memories.

Through it all, we've met amazing nurses, doctors and therapists whose strength and professionalism are unmatched. We've been comforted by friends and family.

And we've learned to be grateful for each day, even the worst ones. If there's one thing childhood cancer has taught our family, it's that these are the good days, the ones that will fill the scrapbook of memory no matter what the future brings.

Next month we travel to Mayo Clinic in Rochester, Minnesota, to meet with the famed medical center's neurological specialists. It's our hope they will give us good news about Amelia's condition and recovery.

My dear Amelia, the angel God has placed in our care, I know I can survive anything as long as I have her.

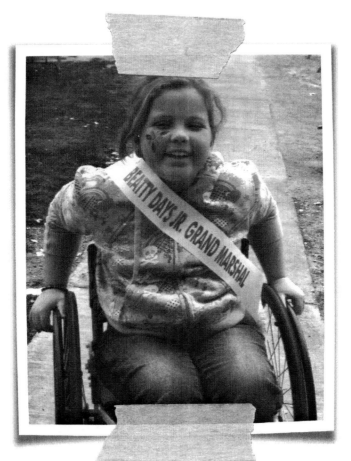

Meet the Junior Grand Marshal.

Amelia's parade

A funny thing happened to the Smiths after we moved back to Las Vegas. Amelia's incandescent spirit and inspiring story caught the attention of people from throughout the community and far beyond.

At work I received e-mails and letters from across the United States and places as far away as England and Japan. Whether through the Internet or by word-of-mouth, the story had gotten out that our miracle child was someone special even among other young people faced with similar life-threatening maladies.

A number of letters came from older people, some in their eighties, who asked Amelia to pray for them so that they might be strong like she was. Other contacts came from people who also had beaten cancer and, like survivors of a great tsunami, wanted to share their own inspiring experiences.

It was a little overwhelming, but Amelia took it all in stride. When she was feeling up to it, we would go to the Target store, a favorite of hers, or out to lunch at a local restaurant. Invariably, strangers would approach her and ask if she was that brave little girl they'd been reading about in the newspaper. She would nod in affirmation, flash a bright smile, and thank them for their kindness and their prayers.

Amelia's story encouraged the kind people of Beatty, located one hundred miles north of Las Vegas, to invite her to be the "Junior Grand Marshal" of the annual Beatty Days Parade. She rode with her folks in a 1915 Coca-Cola red Model T. Our driver was the Model T's proud owner, eighty-year-old Harold Mann. Costumed cowboys and dance hall girls with nicknames like "High Pockets" and "Starr" delighted the crowd by staging more shootouts in two hours than Dodge City saw in twenty years.

Amelia passed out candy and greeted the locals, wearing her "Junior Grand Marshal" sash with pride. Residents approached us and whispered about how impressed they were with her poise. "She's so grown up for such a little thing," they said.

Not long after Beatty Days had ended, Amelia met Holocaust survivor Stephen Nasser, whose book *My Brother's Voice* tells the heart-wrenching true story of his time as a child in a Nazi work camp. Stephen is a wise, soft-spoken man who has inspired many thousands of young people with his amazing life story.

But it was Stephen whose spirits were lifted by reading of Amelia's grace in the face of brain cancer. Her courageous fight reminded him to carry on even after his own grown daughter was silenced by the disease.

"You are the reason I am alive today," Stephen told her. "You are a brave girl who helps others be brave."

***

As the months passed, her condition seemed to improve slowly, if a little unsteadily. Her oncologist in Las Vegas, Dr. Jonathan Bernstein, was pleased with her improvement and the fact she was showing no signs of relapse. But it was clear that the cancer, combined with enormous doses of chemotherapy and radiation, had taken a devastating toll on our child.

She struggled daily, at times suffered miserably, and sometimes was forced to return to the hospital in an attempt to turn back her pain. Somehow, she always came through. Surely by then she knew what was at stake. Her courage was undaunted and awed her friends and family, nurses, and doctors.

And plenty of firefighters, too.

After learning of her amazing story, the Clark County Fire Department and our area volunteers at Station 81 made her an honorary firefighter and issued her an official helmet that remains the envy of the department. Chief Steve Smith (who is not related) made the trip to our community in the mountains outside Las Vegas to make the presentation, and Station 81's resident chief Pat Vannozzi spoke of how our girl's courage had been an inspiration. She was a hero, not only for surviving against long odds, but because of the way she carried herself throughout her ordeal.

✳✳✳

Amelia's spirit manifests its beauty in many ways, not the least of which is her interest in participating in charitable events that help children with cancer and adults who suffer from a variety of challenges.

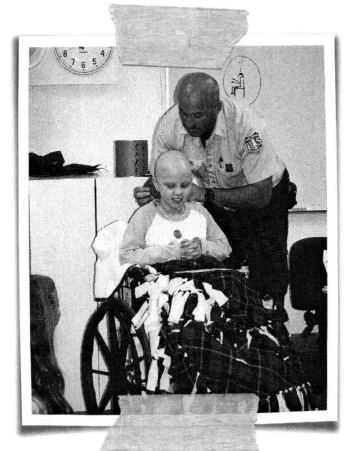

Amelia receives her medal for bravery from
the National Forest Service.

Each winter, "Amelia's Team" dresses in red Santa suits and joins the sea of Clauses in the Great Las Vegas Santa Run to benefit Opportunity Village, a southern Nevada nonprofit that provides jobs and support for mentally challenged adults. She insists on pushing her wheelchair as much as she can over the downtown course.

And there are the numerous fundraising races and walks for the Candlelighters, the Nevada Childhood Cancer Foundation, and the Make-A-Wish Foundation. These charitable foundations provide everything from summer camps and Christmas presents to airline tickets and rent payments for families whose children face catastrophic illness.

She giddily shaves her dad's head each year at the St. Baldrick's Day celebration, a national childhood cancer research fundraiser that is locally headquartered at McMullan's Irish Pub.

Owners Brian and Lynn McMullan, who lost a child to cancer, have taken a keen interest in Amelia's progress.

With a gang of "shavees" and volunteers that grows each year, our group has helped raise nearly a half-million dollars, almost all of which stays in the community to benefit pediatric cancer clinics such as the one by Dr. Jonathan Bernstein. Dr. B, as the children fondly refer to him, works endless hours. He has sacrificed his health and his personal life for the hundreds of children whose lives depend on him. The families of many of those sick kids find their way to his office without insurance, but soon find they will be treated professionally and with respect.

Each year Dr. B is part of the growing numbers who converge on McMullan's to take part in the St. Baldrick's Day fundraiser. The participants and the funds keep growing, and

Amelia is proud to shave her dad's head to help support the charity.

The bruising 2009 recession didn't stop the intrepid characters who gathered for the third annual St. Baldrick's fundraiser. And I do mean characters.

Amelia once again took the electric clippers to my noggin. She's getting good at it: Not a drop of blood was spilled, and I departed with both ears still more or less in place. Event host and NBC television affiliate anchor Kevin Janison gave Amelia high marks for her buzzing skills, and one chair over, Dr Bernstein was treated to a clipping by one of his patients, four-year-old Ethan Freer.

Ethan weaved through the early evening crowd like a halfback with his father, Ben, in constant pursuit. (Ben serves in the 15th Recon Squadron at Creech Air Force Base.) Dressed in his pajamas, with a medical mask dwarfing his sweet face, Ethan was bald before he came through the door of the childhood cancer fundraiser.

Ethan is undergoing treatment for a neuroblastoma tumor by Dr. Bernstein, who is a hero to many of the families in the room, mine included. Ethan was feeling well enough to participate in the event, especially when he learned he would get to help shave the head of his favorite doctor.

With Ben, mother RyAnn, and sisters Brenna and Natalie looking on, Ethan did an excellent job on Dr. B. The child has already undergone eight rounds of chemotherapy. His family remains hopeful and grateful.

"The pediatric oncology world is small," RyAnn said. "You meet these people, and you get to build friendships and relationships. Any time the community supports any one of us, it's just a blessing. It's wonderful to see awareness being raised for pediatric cancer."

Across the generations, but sharing a common spirit, Michael Harvey and his wife, Penny, waited in line to sign in for his shaving. It would be Michael's first since he served as a Marine in the Vietnam era.

"I figure if Amelia can shave your head, I can shave mine," Michael said proudly.

Afterward, Penny kept her sense of humor about her husband's new 'do.

***

Amelia has always been a baseball fan, so when our friends with the Las Vegas 51s Triple-A baseball team invited her to throw out the first pitch at a Chicago Cubs-Seattle Mariners Spring Training game, she immediately began warming up in the family bullpen. With her ravaged legs in a near-constant state of pain, she still had more bad days than good, but as game time approached Amelia couldn't stop smiling.

"Will I be out there on the field?" she asked. "Will I get to keep the baseball? Can I get autographs?"

We arrived three hours early for the noon ballgame, before most of the players for either team, but 51s public relations man Bob Blum and team general manager Don Logan were there to make sure we found our way down to the field. In short order, the players began ambling onto the field to warm up.

Amelia was outfitted with an official baseball and an autograph book, but the players passed by her in a blur. Fortunately, our friend Mary the security guard ushered us toward the dugout, and she introduced us to the Mariners as they jogged by. Several signed her baseball, and a few stopped to politely chat a moment.

I decided not to tell them they were fortunate to be meeting a hero disguised as a twelve-year-old girl.

Then it was our turn to move toward the first-base dugout, where the Cubs came and went in business-like fashion. It was one of the last games of Spring Training, and professional ballplayers can't wait for the regular season to start. Frankly, I didn't expect much more than perfunctory politeness from them.

Instead, Amelia was greeted like a member of their team. I stepped back as All-Stars Carlos Zambrano, Alfonso Soriano, Derrek Lee, and a host of others surrounded her and signed away, giving her a pep talk and slapping high fives. She felt like moving to Chicago immediately.

And when the time came to throw out the first pitch, she threw a strike — and spent the rest of the day marveling at all the autographs she'd collected from her new favorite team.

***

Sometimes just before bed after a long and painful day, Amelia takes a moment to thank her mom and dad for helping to save her life. In reality, it's just the opposite. It is our amazing young girl who has saved her parents' terminally ordinary lives.

"Sooner or later, everybody has some bad things in their life," Amelia told me one night. "I just had it happen when I was young. Even if I never walk again, I'm just so grateful for my life."

Me, too, sweetheart.

Amelia proudly wears her medal for bravery.

207

A Note On Amelia's Charities

When our Amelia was diagnosed with a malignant brain tumor, we were thrust into a world of doctors and difficult decisions. Although family and friends rallied to our side, and strangers contacted us from across the country, we often still felt isolated and at times very much alone.

That's when a group of new friends appeared. They represented the Candlelighters Childhood Cancer Foundation of Nevada, the Make-A-Wish Foundation, and the Nevada Childhood Cancer Foundation. They carried with them gifts for Amelia and a message for us: "You are not alone."

When Amelia was at last out of the hospital, we learned about the St. Baldrick's Foundation and its focus on fund-raising for childhood cancer research. We saw the money raised during its annual day of head shaving stay in our community to help treat children on the front lines of their cancer fight. The message was repeated: "You are not alone."

Thanks in part to the efforts of these charities and other worthy foundations, Amelia received a boost to her spirits at crucial times in her journey. For that, the Smith family will always be grateful.

The message of hope echoes through everything they do.

Shaving the Way to Conquer Kids' Cancer

Despite tremendous progress in research, cancer remains the #1 disease killer of children in the U.S. and Canada. The St. Baldrick's Foundation is an IRS designated 501(c)(3) charity that raises money for childhood cancer research, primarily through head-shaving events. Volunteers, sponsored by family, friends and employers, go bald in solidarity with kids who typically lose their hair during cancer treatment.

Proceeds are granted to the world's leading childhood cancer research institutions. Since 2000, St. Baldrick's has united volunteers in one vision — to fund a cure for every form of childhood cancer, and to ensure each survivor has a high quality of life post-treatment.

To get involved, visit our website at www.StBaldricks.org
or call 888-899-BALD.

because *kids* can't fight cancer alone.

Chartered in 1978, Candlelighters Childhood Cancer Foundation of Nevada was founded by two families, each of whom had a child being treated for cancer. They believed that families could find strength, knowledge and comfort by banding together during difficult times. They wanted to use their experience and resources to lessen the burden of families they knew would follow. Since that time, Candlelighters has assisted more than 2,000 families. Through its many programs, Candlelighters provides assistance for quality-of-life issues that are a large part of the childhood cancer experience, including disease-specific education and emotional support. In certain circumstances, Candlelighters also offers families much-needed financial support. Some of the most vital services Candlelighters provide include: patient advocacy, emergency assistance, travel for treatment, family counseling, survivor scholarships and other programs and services such as meal tickets, hospital visits, toy boxes for out-patient clinics, financial aid guidance, bereavement support and much more.

www.candlelightersnv.org, phone 702-737-1919

MAKE·(A·)WISH.

SOUTHERN NEVADA CHAPTER

The Make-A-Wish Foundation® of Southern Nevada grants the wishes of children with life-threatening medical conditions to enrich the human experience with hope, strength and joy.

Children undergoing long term medical treatment keep busy schedules filled with doctors' appointments, hospital stays, painful and invasive medical procedures. The wish provides moments of wonder and delight to so many children and the families who love them, in need of relief from the daily stresses and uncertainties associated with the diagnosis of a life-threatening medical condition.

"The granting of our daughter's wish was so much more than the materialistic aspect. Although everything we needed was provided by Make-A-Wish, the biggest blessing that you provided for our family us very hard to put into words. The wish gave us a distraction, a goal to look forward to. We were able to take a break and focus on reinforcing our love for each other. We cannot put a price tag on that."

www.snv.wish.org, phone 702-212-9474

Nevada Childhood Cancer Foundation

Since 1993, the Mission of the Nevada Childhood Cancer Foundation has been to work side by side with the medical community to provide social, emotional, educational, financial and psychological support services and programs to families of ALL children diagnosed with a life threatening or critical illness such as cancer, HIV/AIDS, sickle cell, hemophilia, renal disorders and immunologic diseases.

The NCCF is a non-profit organization serving critically ill children and their families living in Southern Nevada and offers over 25 programs and services including the first and only in-patient classroom in the state of Nevada.

The NCCF continues to create new programs and services to fill the voids that exist in helping critically ill children.

Visit NCCF at www.nvccf.org, phone 702-735-8434